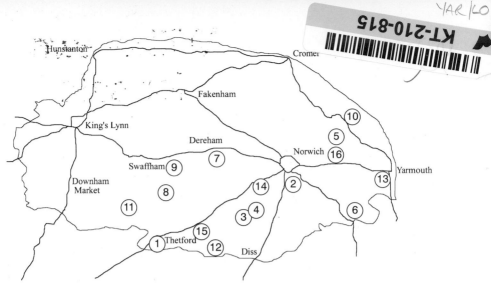

Contents

All map references in this booklet are prefixed with the number of the 1;50,000 Landranger Series of Ordnance Survey maps. The references also apply to the 1;25,000 Pathfinder and Explorer series.

1 – Historic Thetford

6 Miles

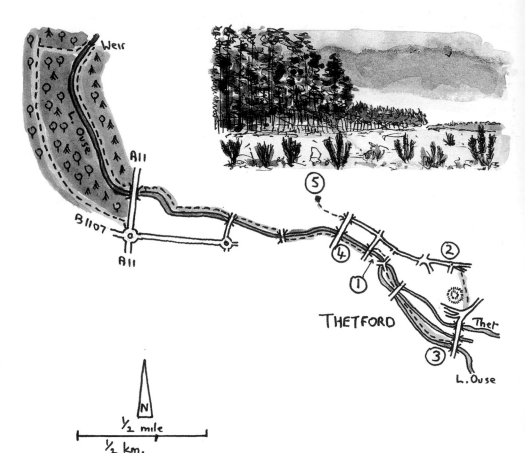

For those who like exercise this walk covers the town and adds some pleasant walking along the Little Ouse and through Thetford Forest. The circular route does not include a visit to the ruins of the 12th century Cluniac Priory but this is remedied by adding a diversion from the Town Bridge at the end of the walk. Start the walk from the Riverside car park close to the Town Bridge and the Bell Hotel. (Ref. 144/870831)

1) Leave the car park by crossing the three-legged bridge heading for the shopping centre. Turn left along the riverside path to the old A11 road. Turn right across the Town Bridge, pass the Bell Hotel and turn right into King Street immediately before St Peter's Church. Shortly on the left is King's House, originally the Shooting Lodge of King James. In front there is the imposing statue of Thomas Paine. The statue, erected in 1964, was designed by Sir Charles Wheeler RA to commemorate the life of this son of Thetford. The author of "Rights of Man" played a role in the American and French Revolutions before he was hounded out of England for daring to tell ordinary people that they had rights. Look at the statue and ponder why the book Paine is holding is upside down. Continue along King Street, past St Cuthbert's Church, to the Market Place.. Cross the Market Place and carry on ahead along Castle Street.

2) Cross over the mini roundabout and enter the cul de sac to the right of the trees. Turn right into Castle Park and pass the earthworks of the Iron Age defences from 500 BC to arrive alongside Castle Hill. Follow the path across the park and turn right into Old Market Street. Behind the high flint wall on the left is Thetford's Forgotten Garden. The garden had become overgrown before being restored as a public space. Leave the Dolphin Inn to the right and take the left fork followed almost at once by another left turn towards Nun's Bridges. Cross the first bridge over the River Thet and the second bridge over a stream and turn right before the third bridge over the Little Ouse.

3) Follow Spring Walk along the river bank passing Spring House on the right. Cross over a small bridge onto the site of an old mill, known locally as The Coffee Mill. At a cross path turn right towards the town centre and then left onto Burren Island. At the end of the Island is the statue of The Maharajah Duleep Singh. Duleep Singh was the last Sikh Maharajah of the Punjab. Continue on to the left part of the three-legged bridge and return to the car park.

Follow the riverside path over the Town Bridge, where it is renamed the Haling Path, as it now heads out of town heading towards Brandon.

4) Walk under the bridge that carries London Road over the river and continue to the Blaydon Bridge. This bridge was erected in 1970 and named after George Richard Blaydon who made a generous donation towards its cost. Cross over the bridge, turn left and carry on along the Little Ouse path. Go under the Canterbury Way Bridge and the newer A11 bypass bridges and carry on alongside the river and the fishing lakes. At Abbey Heath Weir cross the river, turn left back along the bank for a short distance and then turn right across a footbridge into Thetford Forest. Carry on along a clear but muddy track through the wood to a clearing. At the clearing turn left along a forest edge track. At a junction of paths bear left through a small wooded area onto another open space. At the next path junction bear left towards the traffic on the road in the distance. Where the path meets the main road walk a short distance to the right and climb the road bank onto the B1107 at the junction with the A11. Cross the A11 at the roundabout with care and carry on along the B1107 towards the town centre. At a mini roundabout turn left along Canterbury Way to the River Bridge. Cross the bridge and take the path on the right down to the riverside path. Follow the path back to the Town Bridge and the car park.

5) To visit the Cluniac Priory from the Town Bridge walk past the Bell Hotel and turn left along Minstergate. Go through the underpass and into the priory car park. The priory, dating from 1107, was the most important of the town's religious houses. In medieval times pilgrims visited the famous Lady Chapel seeking its miraculous healing powers. The sheer size if the ruins and the pleasant open spaces make this a well worthwhile visit.

2 – Shotesham Five Churches

6½ Miles

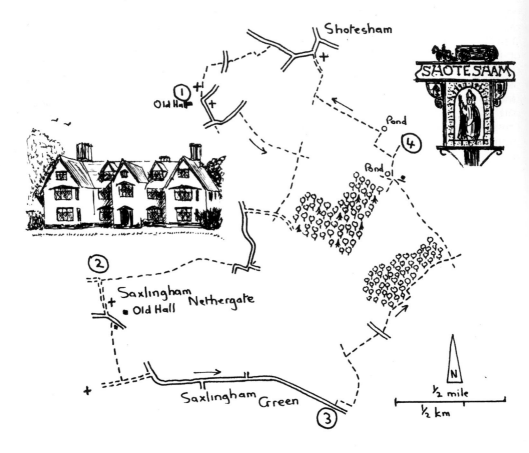

1) From Shotesham St Mary's Church car park, (Ref. 134/247990) and with the church behind you, turn left into the road and walk past the second, ruined and ivy-covered church on your left. Carry on to the T-junction with Rogers Lane. Ignore the FP sign ahead. Turn left and walk a few yards to a FP sign on the right. Turn right and walk along a field edge track. (The path bends left at a waymarker and rustic seat). Keep following this path until you reach a crossing footpath. Turn right and walk across the field to a stile or if there is a field edge path, follow it round to the left to reach the waymarked plank bridge and a stile. The owners of this land are leaving field edges for walkers as part of a Countryside Stewardship scheme. Cross the stile and walk ahead on the right hand side of the field. Cross the stile in the right hand corner at the end of the field, and turn right along a farm track to the road. Turn left and walk along the road, Wood Lane. Follow the road right just after the junction with Wash Lane (there is a footbridge if water is flowing across the road) to a footpath sign ahead. Take the field edge path from the corner of the road making sure that you cross a stile into a meadow near its end. At the far end of this meadow is another stile on the left. Cross the stile and turn left into Saxlingham Nethergate churchyard.

2) Follow the path on the right hand side. Pass by the church (which is usually open) and walk out to the road ahead. It is worth looking round this pretty village with its splendid Old Hall, near the church entrance. Cross the road and immediately through the small gate ahead (not signposted) into Saxlingham School. The path continues straight ahead past school buildings to another gate out of the school grounds and into a field. Continue straight on, over a plank bridge, until you reach a crossing track. At this point, turn right to visit Saxlingham St Mary Magdelene ruined church inside a small wood. Come back to the track, retrace your steps and continue ahead to a road. Turn right (joining a local trail called Boudica's Way – note the yellow waymark bearing a sword) and walk along the road to a sharp right hand bend with a minor road straight ahead signposted to Shotesham and Brooke. Continue along the minor road (Saxlingham Green) using the very wide verges where possible to another Boudica's Way waymark on the left.

3) Turn left into a field and immediately right on to a field edge path. Follow this round the field, turning right at the Boudica's Way sign, and keeping on in the same direction until you meet a minor road. Cross the road and pick up a cross-field path on the other side which goes to the edge of Little Wood. Turn right and follow Boudica's Way round the edge of the wood to a stile on the left, cross this and still keeping the wood on your left, walk on until you come to a stile a little hidden away at the northernmost tip of the wood. Cross the stile and continue forward across a field to a grassy track leading to Stubbs Green, passing a white cottage on your right in due course. Continue ahead to a pond, ignoring all other signposts. Turn right at the pond and follow a hedge on your left to a gap with a footbridge across a ditch into the next field. (Do not go as far as the footbridge ahead that can be seen more clearly than the one on the left).

4) Cross the field to a newly-planted hedge, turn right to a pond, then left across another field to the edge of a wood (you are still on Boudica's Way). Keep ahead on a grassy track looking forward at a fine view of Shotesham St Mary's Church, to a crossing steam where you must turn right at the side of the wood. This path takes you over a stream to emerge at Roger's Lane and Shotesham All Saints' Church. The walk turns left at Rogers Lane, but first visit the church that is set on high ground behind you. There are fine views across Shotesham Common from this vantagepoint. Walk along Rogers Lane and take the first turning on the right (Priory Lane). Continue ahead to footpath on the left opposite some bungalows. Turn left on to the footpath and follow it over a minor road towards St Mary's Church and the car park.

3 – Old and New Buckenhams

6½ Miles

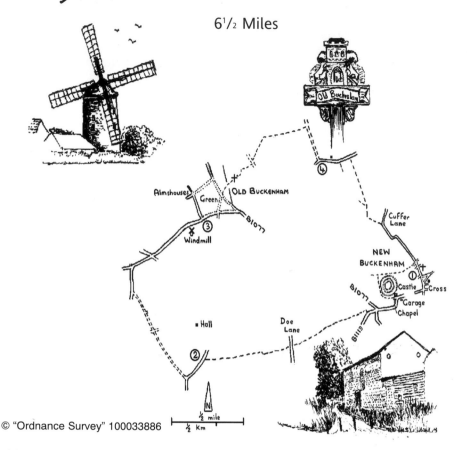

© "Ordnance Survey" 100033886

This walk starts in the centre of New Buckenham (Ref. 144/088905) close to the small village green and market cross, please be careful parking your vehicle to avoid inconvenience to local people.

1) Follow the lane to the left of the Post Office/shop, pass the church, to the small cross roads with Moat Lane right (leading to village hall) and St Martin's Gardens left. Take a footpath alongside St Martin's Gardens, continue along field edges then beside the moat around New Buckenham Castle, join a track, pass the bridge and gate into the castle, then out to the road.

From outside the castle you see little more than the fine moat, but if you go inside it is

hard to believe the impressive earthworks and the ruins of the keep are so well hidden. The William de Albini, who built the Norman castle, married the widow of Henry I, and the family were closely involved with many events in English history.

Key and information from Castle Hill Garage (fee payable, adults £1) Closed Thursday 1 p.m. plus all day summertime Mondays and wintertime Sundays. Close to the road visible remains of St Mary's Chapel, are incorporated into a barn – recently converted into holiday accommodation, the sketch shows it as it was.

Our route takes us to the right along the road (B1113), keep to the right, soon reaching the B1077 cross roads, go straight ahead for a short distance, then just in front of a large road sign turn right and quickly bear left behind gardens. Keep to the left edges, going over five stiles then into a grassy track, then three more stiles and out to Doe Lane. Go across and continue along the left edge, ahead into the next field, bear left round a pond then over a footbridge, turn right and follow the right edges, firstly through a young copse then along a field edge, join a track and out to a road, turn left.

2) Follow the road bending gently right, then, as it swings left, turn sharp right along a track. Follow to end, ignoring all turnings. Turn right along the road and at a T-junction go right again. At X-junction go straight ahead, passing the windmill to the green.

The very large mill is being restored, a new cap and sails have been fitted in recent years, interior restoration is ongoing; it is open to the public on the second Sunday of each month during the summer from 2pm to 5pm.

3) Choose your route across or around the large green. Turning left along the westerly edge will provide a view of the almshouses. For the direct route go ahead along the south side of the green, then left at a crossroad. On reaching the B1077 cross and follow a short lane to All Saints Church. Just left of the church rooms a gate leads into the churchyard.

The church has an unusual octagonal tower and a thatched roof. There is a Norman doorway in the north wall, a number of 13th century features and each century since has made a contribution.

Go either side of the church to the opposite corner of the churchyard, keep left through an extension of the grave-yard, then over a stile into a field. The top rail of the stile lifts up to allow easy access (best if one person holds the rail while another climbs over)

these stiles are designed so the horses will not be injured on projecting steps. Go across the field, over another stile, through rails and turn left on a green track. In a few yards go right over a stile by a gate, diagonally across the field to go over another stile, then through a gap in the hedge, turn right and over a footbridge.

Go ahead along the right edges of two fields to a track, turn right to a road and then turn left.

4) Pass a modern house on the left, continue for a further 200 metres, then turn right along a field edge path. (This concessionary path is used as an alternative to the definitive right of way starting 150m to the west, the two routes meet about two thirds of the way along.) Follow the left edge, go over a footbridge, continue your direction to go over a stile to the right of a gate. Go diagonally across the field to a stile and a gate by a transformer on a post. Turn right on Cuffer Lane, and follow it back into New Buckenham.

If you have not already done so you may wish to explore the village, the street pattern still reflects the streets of the original town, which grew up around the new Norman castle built around 1150 so New Buckenham has been 'new' for about 850 years! Interestingly the castle is still within the parish boundary of Old Buckenham, (the site of the old castle alongside Abbey Road, Old Buckenham was used for the Augustinian priory, most of which was pulled down after the Dissolution and the remains incorporated into Abbey Farm.) St Martin's Church dates from the mid 13th century, when the population grew too large for St Mary's Chapel, but much of the present building dates from the 15th and 16th centuries. New Buckenham has many houses and cottages dating back several hundred years in addition to the 16th century Market Cross on the green.

4 – Bunwell

7 Miles

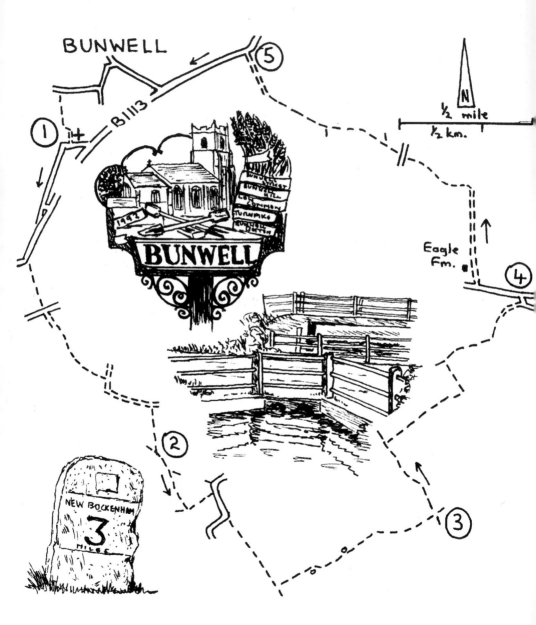

BUNWELL

B1113

Eagle Fm.

BUNWELL

NEW BUCKENHAM 3 MILES

½ mile
½ km.

N

① ② ③ ④ ⑤

This walk starts from Bunwell Church (Ref. 144/125927), just off B1113. Some of our rights of way are very old, a link with our history, they are ancient monuments, maybe just as valuable and important as some vertical structures. It is a delight to follow pathways which may not have changed very greatly in hundreds of years.

1) From Bunwell Church go westwards, then south, following the old road by-passed by The Turnpike. Near the end turn left then cross the main road and continue southwards along the verge. As the road bends to the right fork left on a bridleway and follow the field edge. Cross a lane and go ahead along a hedged track, then a field edge. Turn right at a T-junction and soon left. These ancient tracks, from the junction with the modern B road, are shown as a road on Faden's map of 1797 and were probably already old then. Follow the track, which appears to coincide with an ancient boundary, for about 350 yards, turn right over a stile and go straight down the field edge.

2) Continue to the bottom of the field go over a footbridge and stiles then turn left to soon cross another stile and a bridge. Bear left with the path, do not go into the field immediately ahead, but bear right and then out into a field. Follow the field edge until you almost reach a crossing track swinging round ahead of you. Turn sharp left to go down steps, over a footbridge and a stile and continue to a road and turn right. When the road swings to the right go ahead on a footpath until you reach the corner of a field. Turn left over a stile then right continuing your previous line with a hedge on your right. At the second crossing field boundary turn left with hedge on your right. Follow the boundary, passing two ponds (at the second one the path goes between the hedge and the pond) then at a field corner go over a stile on your right then turn left to continue your previous line across an open field. Go across a bridge then follow the line of isolated trees, the remnant of an old hedge, for about 200 yards.

3) Turn left across the field towards the external corner of a hedged boundary (just to the right of the corner there is a gap with a large tree in the centre). Beyond the corner, and a little to the left, a waymark is visible in a further hedge, the next point to aim for following the field edge. Cross a bridge, continue ahead along a field edge to a corner, turn right over a bridge, then ahead on a broad track along a field edge (the right of way is about 50 yards to your left in mid field, but eventually joins the field edge). At the end of the second field turn left on a track then right on a broader track.

4) On reaching the road turn left twice. After about 300 yards turn right along the drive of Eagle Farmhouse and go straight ahead in a green lane. At the end of the lane go left through a gap and follow the field edge, at the end of the field go ahead over a footbridge into a hedged lane. Cross a road and take the footpath ahead, following the field edge. Go ahead over a bridge, ignoring bridge on your right, and follow the watercourse, a tributary of the River Tas, until, with a house just in view ahead, the track swings to the left towards a gap. Go into a hedged lane on the right of the gap and follow through to the road.

5) Turn left along the verge for about 600 yards, go right on a minor road signed "Bunwell 1", turn left along road signed "Church", then turn right along Barham's Lane. Just before a ford across the lane turn left on a clear path towards the church, pass a playing field and school, note the attractive plaque commemorating the school's centenary, and back to the starting point.

5 – Thurne and the Broads

7 Miles

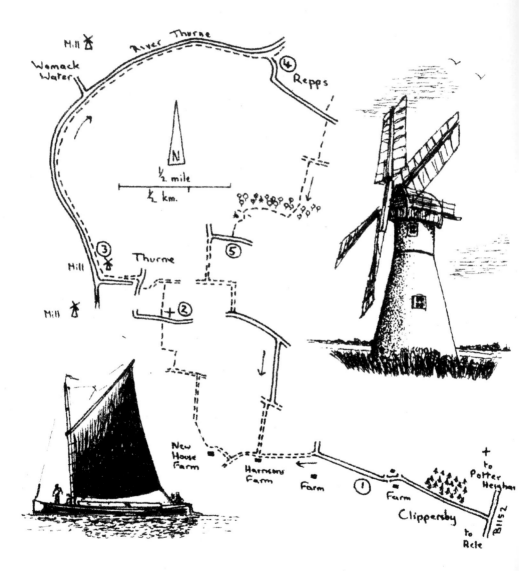

River Thurne

Mill

Womack Water

Repps ④

½ mile

½ km.

N

Thurne ⑤

③ Hill

Mill ②

New House Farm

Harrisons Farm

Farm

① Farm

Clippersby

to Potter Heigham

B1152

to Acle

This walk takes in the attractive village of Thurne with its two wind pumps, complete with sails, and follows the Weavers Way along the River Thurne to Repps. This river is a favourite for sailing boats and on occasions it is possible to see a Norfolk Wherry on this stretch.

1) The start of the walk is at a small roadside car park just to the west of Clippesby village. (Ref. 134/419145) Clippesby is to the west of the B1152 Potter Heigham to Acle road about a mile north of the junction of the B1152 and the A1064. A signboard at the car park indicates that it is the starting place for a permissive path leading to the River Bure. From the car park follow the road west as far as a road junction. At the junction go straight ahead down the farm road to the farm buildings. Go between the buildings of Harrisons Farm and take the road to the left just past the farmhouse. In 100 yards turn right along Weavers Way which is along the road to New House Farm. Keep to the right of the farm buildings and follow the signs around the buildings and across the field to the right. At the end of the field the path turns right along a grassy track to a concrete road. Turn left along the road to the entrance of the caravan park. From this point there are fine views of the church, wind pumps and sailing boats on the river. Turn right and in 100 yards turn left between trees for a short distance and follow the path to the right towards the church.

2) The thatched church is dedicated to St Edmund the King Martyr. Take the path off the tarmac road to the west of the church and follow the path over two stiles to the road. Turn left along the concrete road and follow it round to the left through brick farm buildings. The path joins the road in the village centre. Turn right past the shop and toilets towards Ramblers' gift shop. Turn left alongside the marina to join the riverside path to the old drainage mill.

3) Thurne Dyke Drainage Mill was built in 1820 and has been restored complete with sails. Follow the riverside path (Weavers Way) as it bears around in a large right hand sweep, past the entrance to Wormack Water, as far as Repps. The path leaves the riverbank and follows a concrete path behind riverside chalets. At the road leading to the marina turn right along Staithe Road into the village.

4) Follow the tarmac road as it winds through the village. Pass by Hall Farm, with its brick buildings, and in 100 yards (just before the next houses on the left and opposite a footpath sign on the left) go through a hole in the hedge to a crossfield path on the right. Cross the first field to a grassy track and pick up the fingerpost a few yards to the right pointing left across the second field to the corner of the woods ahead. Follow the line of the path along the right edge of the woods to the corner of the field and take the path over a footbridge on the right into the woods. Go through the wood, over a bridge to the far side and turn right, just inside the wood, along a grassy track. Follow the path, past the farm buildings on the left, as far as the farm gates. Cross the broad path leading to the farm from the right and take the path straight ahead with a hedge to the right. Follow the path, along the field edge, to the right of the house ahead. Go right through a gateway and left to the road.

5) Follow the tarmac road to the right and, where the road turns right, turn left along a grassy track. At the end of the field take the left path leading away from the church. At the corner of the field take the right turn across the field edge to the road. Turn left along the road, past School Farm, to the road junction. Turn right along the road and at the next junction turn right and almost immediately left along the road to Harrison's Farm. At the farm turn left between the buildings and follow the farm road and lane back to the starting point.

6 – Beccles and Gillingham

7½ Miles

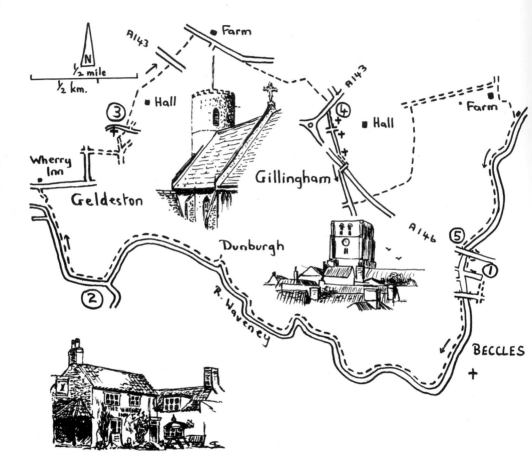

© "Ordnance Survey" 100033886

The walk starts at the Tourist Information Centre on Beccles Quay. Park in the large free car park a few yards further along the Quay (Ref. 134/423912)

1) From the Visitor Centre walk towards the Town Centre for 100 yards to a crossroads.

Turn right to cross the old Town Bridge and immediately over the bridge turn left along the riverside footpath. Go through the boatyard and over a stile by a 5-bar gate. Follow the boardwalk alongside the moorings.

At the edge of the town the path changes direction to north-westerly and the trees often obscure the river. Follow this grassy path for about 2 miles keeping to the riverbank and ignoring a path to the right at Dunburgh. Just past a derelict boathouse a canal joins the River Waveney. Turn right and follow the canal bank into Geldeston.

2) The Geldeston Dyke was originally built to link the village of Geldeston with the rivers of the Broads. Go under the old railway bridge and continue along the path. At the boatyard take the gravel drive to the right and turn left along the tarmac road to the Wherry Inn. Turn right along the road keeping to the pavement. In 250 yards turn left along Heath Road. In 200 yards, at the brow of the hill, take a grass footpath to the right. At Farthing Green turn left along a broad track and in 40 yards keep left where the path forks. Enter the churchyard by a kissing gate. Geldeston Church is one of about 200 round-towered churches to be found in Norfolk and Suffolk. In 1814 the tower became unsafe and two of the three bells were sold for £50 to pay for the top 16-ft. of the tower to be demolished and rebuilt 4ft lower. A local rhyme rebukes the parish for selling the bells so that the bell tower could be repaired to hold them!

3) Leave the churchyard through a kissing gate onto the road and turn right. Cross the road and go through an iron gate to the left of the Hall entrance. Cross the grass field heading to the left of a wooden stockade on the other side of the field. Go through the gap between the stockade and two old Oak trees. Cross the next field heading for a gap in the wood about 50 yards to the left of a large Oak tree. Go through the gap to a stile to join the A143. Cross the road and take the footpath opposite across a field to Rectory Road. Turn right along the road, past Winston Game Farm, and shortly after passing under the overhead electric cables take a footpath on the right at a point where the road bears left. Follow the path diagonally across the field to a clump of trees in the opposite corner. Go through a gap in the hedge into the next field and in 20 yards turn right through a gap onto a grass path to the left. Follow the path to the main road. Turn left along the road and in 20 yards cross over into a layby by a white post and rail.

4) The route now follows the old road to Beccles now replaced by the new A146. Behind high trees to the left lies the ivy-clad ruins of All Saints Church. Immediately past this is St Mary's Church Gillingham and just a little further along the road is the brick Catholic Church of Our Lady of Perpetual Succour. The A146 bypass cuts off all of these churches from the rest of the village. Take the path and the footbridge over the bypass into Gillingham village. Carry on ahead along the Dam Road past the village hall and immediately past the bus-shelter take the footpath on the left alongside a cottage. Cross the main road and take the footpath straight ahead. Follow the clearly waymarked path as it winds across the marshes. At a farm track turn right heading in the direction of a beautiful ornate barn. To the left of the track there are a number of very old oak trees. At the farm buildings carry on ahead along a concrete road and at the road carry on ahead along a cinder track. Follow the track as it bears right past a pond and at the corner of the farm buildings bear left and follow the path downhill towards the river. Just before Boathouse Hill Cottages turn right over a stile and follow the path half left to a stile. Turn right along the riverbank and follow the path as far as the new bridge over the river.

5) Immediately before the bridge take the path to the right leading to the road. At the road turn left to cross the river and at the lay-by take the path left down to the river. Turn left through the bridge and follow the path around the Yacht Basin to the starting point.

7 – Mattishall

7½ Miles

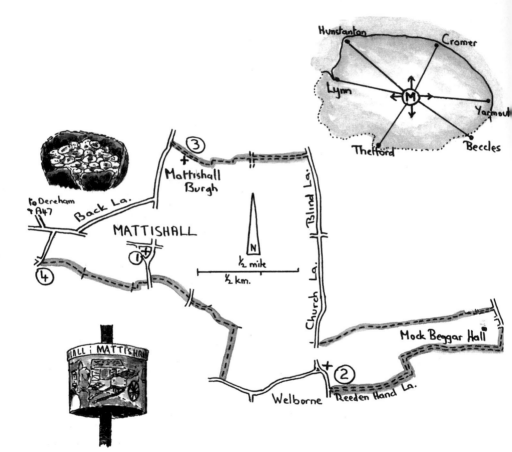

To Dereham & A47 · Back La. · MATTISHALL · Mattishall Burgh · Blind La. · Church La. · Mock Beggar Hall · Welborne · Reeden Hand La.

Hunstanton · Cramer · Lynn · M · Yarmout · Thetford · Beccles

N · ½ mile · ½ km.

① ② ③ ④

HALL : MATTISHA

There is an old joke that Dereham graveyard is the "Dead Centre" of Norfolk. This is disputed by the inhabitants of Mattishall, just four miles away, who claim that their village is the geographical centre of the county. Mattishall is part of the Eight Parishes Project who, collectively, celebrate the life of Parson Woodforde of Weston Longville with well maintained and signed footpaths. This walk uses many of those paths to visit the neighbouring hamlets of Welborne and Mattishall Burgh. Start the walk at the small parking area just to the south of All Saints Church (Ref. 133/053111)

1) From the parking area turn right and walk along Mill Street. At Mill House on the left take the signed footpath through the garden of the house to the open field beyond. At the back of the house note the base of the old windmill which gave the house and street its name. Follow the path through the fields to cross New Lane and continue along the track straight ahead. Part way along the track bear right and eventually go through a gap in the hedge. Turn right along a field edge path to meet a tarmac road. Turn left into Welborne Village. Welborne is a tiny village of only 100 inhabitants but still has its own identity and an annual arts festival. At a bend keep left along Church Road and follow the road to the Church. Welborne Church is one of Norfolk's Round Tower Churches. There are about 200 such churches in Norfolk and Suffolk, more than the total of such churches to be found in the rest of the country. A look at the flint tower will immediately identify one reason for the round structure. Flint is not a suitable building material for corners and so flint buildings have to use brick or limestone wherever a firm edge is required, for example around windows and doors. Square towers would also need considerable quantities of corner material so this is avoided by building towers without corners.

2) After a look at the church continue the walk along the road, signposted Barnham Broom, leaving the cemetery on the left. In a short distance turn left and keep left, along a bridleway, Reeden Hand Lane, and follow this for about a mile to a firm road. Turn left and keep straight ahead at the junction with the major road by Mock Beggar Hall. In 200 yards turn left along the footpath following the drive of Bracken Wood House. Follow the waymarked signs through the buildings and leave by a galvanised gate into a green lane. Go through a sliding rail gate and follow the path winding around the field margins. Keep on the signed path for about a mile to eventually meet Church Lane. Turn right along the tarmac road and follow it, over a crossroad, to a green lane on the left of Blind Lane. In about a quarter of a mile the path meets a cross path, Bullam's Cross Lane. Turn left and almost immediately right onto a field edge path. Keep on the path to Mattishall Burgh Church. This is the third church encountered on this short walk and it is only half a mile from the large church at Mattishall (and not much further from yet another church at North Tuddenham). The reasons for the large numbers of churches may be in part due to the vanity of small communities in wanting their own place of worship or may be due to the much larger rural population when farming was much more labour intensive.

3) Pass the church to the right and carry on along the path to the main road. Turn left along the road and follow it for about quarter of a mile to Back Lane on the right. Walk along Back Lane to the main road and turn right. Just a small distance from here one of Mattishall's claims to fame occurred. In 1968 workmen digging in a development turned up a hoard of about 1100 Roman Silver coins. The coins dated from 145 AD to 260 AD and are now displayed in Norwich Castle Museum. Pass shops on the left and turn left along Welgate. Immediately opposite the road to Ivy Way look for the narrowest of entrances to a footpath adjacent to Ebeneezer Cottage.

4) Follow the path around the edge of a field, cross a narrow footbridge and continue along the well-used path as far as a group of houses. Take the signed path between houses onto the estate road. Turn right and keep onto the road to join Mill Street once more. Turn left along Mill Street to return to the car park.

8 – Watton and Thompson

7½ Miles

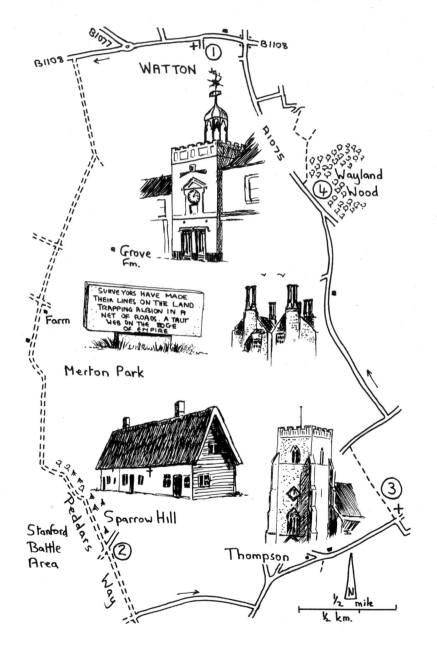

B1077

B1108

B1108

WATTON

①

B1108

B1077

④ Wayland Wood

Grove Fm.

SURVEYORS HAVE MADE THEIR LINES ON THE LAND TRAPPING ALBION IN A NET OF ROADS. A TAUT WEB ON THE EDGE OF EMPIRE

Farm

Merton Park

Sparrow Hill

Stanford Battle Area

Peddars Way

②

③

Thompson

N

½ mile

½ km.

The walk starts at the car park just south of the main street in Watton (Ref. 144/916007) next to the Methodist Church. It follows the Peddars Way for several miles and then visits the village of Thompson before returning via Wayland Wood, reputed to be the site of the Babes in the Wood tale.

1) Leave the car park and turn left towards Swaffham past the old Watton Brewery and the police station. In 3/4 mile keep straight ahead at a roundabout onto Brandon Road. Pass Stokes Avenue on the left and in 100 yards turn left onto the bridleway signed "Peddars Way". In 1/2 mile cross the stream and take the path to the right keeping the hedge to the right. At the end of the hedge carry on ahead towards a clump of trees on the horizon. The barns and thatched roof of Grove Farm are visible across a field to the left. At a cross path carry on ahead onto the Peddars Way (the path already used is an alternative for bridleway users). Keep on the gravel path lined by over mature oaks, past farm buildings and a small flint cottage, until the path comes into the open spaces of Merton Park. Here the Peddars Way leaves the main path, which bends round to the left, and is signed straight ahead along a grass track. Follow the path, with the Stanford Battle Area to the right, for a further mile to a tarmac road "Sparrow Hill".

2) Cross the road and keep on the Peddars Way for a further 1/2 mile, as it follows the line of the old Roman Road, to the next tarmac road. Turn left along the tarmac road and in just over 1/2 mile turn left at the road junction into Thompson Village. At the first junction keep right passing on front of an attractive thatched house. In 100 yards at a further junction keep right once more. The village green, with its duck pond and picnic area, is on the left. Pass the school on the left and at the road junction keep straight ahead along Church Road as far as Thompson Church.

3) Thompson Church is one of the finest examples of the "Decorated" style in East Anglia. It is obvious that the size and importance of this church owes more to its past than its present. It was endowed as a Collegiate Church in 1650 with a community of 6 priests living at College Farm. Take the footpath on the left immediately before the churchyard and follow it to the tarmac road. Turn right and in 1/4 mile turn left along a byway. In about a mile pass Silverdell with extensive gardens and impressive chimneys. Go past the turning on the left and carry onto the main A1075. Cross the busy road and walk to the left for 200 yards with no pavement. Pass the entrance to Wayland Wood and take the signed path to the right along the wood edge.

4) Wayland Wood is reputed to be the site of the Babes in the Wood episode. A great oak was said to mark the spot where the children laid. It was struck by lightning and destroyed in August 1879. It is most probable that the story was based on an event in 1562. The owner of Griston Hall died leaving the Merton Estates to his 7-year-old son. His "Wicked Uncle", who would inherit the estate if the boy died intestate, looked after the boy. At the age of 11 the boy died on the way home from a visit to his stepmother, possibly whilst passing through Wayland Woods. The wicked uncle inherited the estate and the local people raised the cry of foul play. Later the uncle was imprisoned and so was punished as in all good fairy tales!

At the end of the wood and caravan site cross the stile and continue across the field with the hedgerow to the right. In the corner of the field cross the stile on the right and follow the path with the hedge on the left. Take the path as it enters left between hedges and then runs alongside gardens, over a stile and between more houses to enter a housing estate. Turn left and follow Abbey Road, turn right into Vicarage Walk and left along Monktons Drive to the main road. Turn right along the main road to the traffic lights. Turn left along the main street passing by the Clock-house on the right. The Clock-house is the oldest building in the town and was erected after the town was destroyed by fire in 1674. Continue along the street to the car park.

9 - Holme Hale

8 Miles

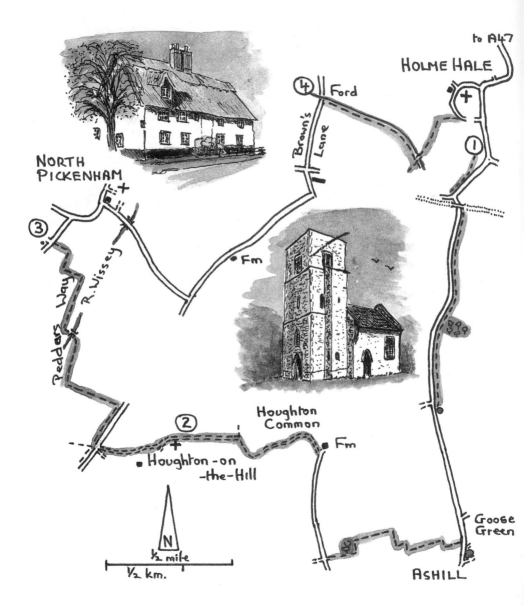

to A47

HOLME HALE

④ Ford

Brown's Lane

NORTH PICKENHAM

①

③

Peddars Way

R. Wissey

• Fm

② Houghton Common

+ Houghton-on -the-Hill

• Fm

N
½ mile
½ km.

Goose Green

ASHILL

What makes an eight mile walk into a really memorable ramble? What about good paths well signed, co-operative landowners allowing permissive access across their land, good views, something special to visit on the way and a pub to refresh the weary traveller. This walk takes in the beautiful Church of Saint Mary, Houghton on the Hill and passes by the Blue Lion at North Pickenham, one of the regular stopping places for those walking the length of the Peddars Way. All of the paths are easy to use and there are excellent views of the surrounding countryside for most of journey. The walk starts at the Holme Hale Pavilion on the junction of the North Pickenham Road and the Hale Road (Ref. 144/889071)

1) From the pavilion car park cross the playing field to the opposite corner and turn right along a grass field edge path. Immediately there are views of the two turbines, the Church and the water tower at Swaffham and the Church at Necton. Leave the field to go left onto the Ashill Road and through the disused railway bridge. Once through the bridge follow the road using the Stewardship path just inside the hedge on the left and stay on this path until it runs out and then continue along the road into Ashill village. Pass the houses on the left as far as the large open space of Goose Green. Take the footpath on the right, opposite the green, signposted between The Old Bakery and Seymore Cottage. Follow the clear path along field edges as far as a tarmac road. Turn right along the road to the farm at Houghton Common. Houghton means "High Place" and again the views from here are spectacular. The later naming of the village "Houghton on the Hill" is therefore tautology, a not infrequent occurrence in place names. Carry on straight-ahead onto a green lane that bears left and continues along field edges to an unsigned large gap in the hedge on the left. Take this green lane as far as the ruins of St Marys Church. The medieval village of Houghton on the Hill has long since disappeared. Is the ten yard wide green lane a clue to its disappearance? This was the width of many droves left between fields during the inclosures of the eighteenth and early ninetieth centuries. Inclosure meant that the landowner changed his farming from the open strip system to sheep farming. The result was the loss of employment for many and the subsequent loss of many small villages.

2) Much has been written about the discovery of this ruined church of St Mary by Bob Davy and the effort he has put into its restoration over the past 14 years. Without his intervention one of the finest examples of a medieval painted church may have been demolished and lost forever. This site has been in turn a Stone Age flint works, an Iron Age settlement, a Roman Villa and a ruin used for devil worship. To see the interior of the church it is necessary to telephone Bob on 01760 440470 and make prior arrangements. However, if you do turn up unexpectedly, the chances are that he will be working somewhere around the church and will be happy to show the visitor around. After visiting the church continue along the lane to the tarmac road. Turn right along the lane and then left along a field edge to follow the Peddars Way. Follow the well waymarked route across fields to meet a tarmac road at the edge of North Pickenham Village.

3) On the opposite side of the road at this point is a memorial to the Men of the USAAF who flew from North Pickenham Airfield in1944-5. Turn right along the road and right at the T-junction to the Blue Lion Inn. Turn right in front of the pub and walk along Houghton Lane to the next road junction. Turn left along the next road and follow this for a little over half a mile to the site of Holme Hale Railway Station. Shortly past the station cross over the main road and follow Brown's Lane to a ford.

4) Just before the ford turn right along a permissive path. In just under half a mile turn left at a cross path, go over a footbridge and follow the path to the road in the village. Turn left along the road and follow it round to the right to Holme Hale Church and a pretty thatched cottage. Keep ahead to the next road. Turn right and follow the road back to the starting point.

10 – Potter Heigham

8 Miles

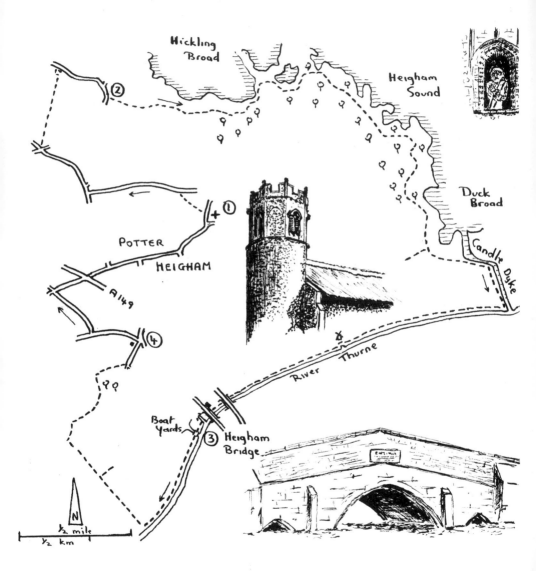

The walk starts at Potter Heigham Church. Park on the small triangle of grass outside the Church (Ref. 134/419199) The first part and the end of the walk are across fields where the paths are not always well maintained. The rest of the walk follows the Weavers Way around Hickling Broad and the River Thurne.

1) Potter Heigham Church is undoubtedly one of the most beautiful churches in the County with its Round Tower (once a Beacon), thatched roof and hammer beams. Over the south door a sculpture sits in a niche. The statue is variously called a Green Man or a Man of Life and is probably of Pagan origin pre dating the church. Start the walk along Church Lane to the west of the church. Just past the church tower take the footpath on the left across a field. Go through the gap in the hedge and across the next field to join the road. Turn left along the road to a T-junction with a thatched bungalow on the left. Turn right and follow the road to the crossroads. At the crossroads take the footpath half-right ahead and follow the waymark on the electricity post across the field. Follow the line of trees heading for buildings on the horizon. At a large oak tree at the edge of the field turn left for a few yards and follow the signs through the garden of the house onto the road. Turn right along the road. The road bears right and after 100 yards pick up the path onto Weavers Way by a five bar gate on the left.

2) For the next two miles the route follows the Weavers Way through Hickling Broad, a national nature reserve covering 1200 acres, including all of Hickling Broad and Heigham Sound. The path winds among reed beds with tantalising views of sailing boats, windpumps and thatched buildings. The giant wind turbine, and the farm of smaller turbines, at Winterton appear at intervals along the route. The path leaves the wooded area by a stile and comes into more open country. In 400 yards the old route of the Weavers Way, along an old railway track, is on the right. Ignore this and continue to follow the Candle Dyke to its junction with the River Thurne. Follow the path to the right along the river. The path passes by a modern pumping station drawing the water out of the fens into the river and almost immediately passes by a now sail-less wind pump (High's Mill) that performed the same function in the past. The path goes under the bridge carrying the bypass and comes to the old bridge probably built about 1385 before the days of pleasure boats using the Broads. The Broadshaven Tavern offers refreshment before crossing the road and wending a way around the boatyard to rejoin the path along the riverbank.

3) Cross the boatyard entrance by a footbridge and follow the concrete path, behind the riverside chalets, to its end. Take the footpath to the right through trees and bushes. Ignore the first path to the right and continue along the path to a ditch. Cross the ditch and turn right along a field edge. Follow the path around the field edges to a point about 150 yards short of the A1062 where the path crosses into a wood by a footbridge. Walk through the wood and turn left along the tarmac road to join the A1062. Turn left past (or into) the Falgate Inn along the road and into Market Road on the right. Turn right along the byroad as far as the A149. Cross the road and go through the barriers of the blocked off road opposite. Keep straight ahead at the road junction , past the school and follow the road back to the church. Just before the church the attractive Bethal Farm, with its thatched barns, indicates the former prosperity of this parish.

11 – Santon Downham and Brandon

8³/₄ Miles

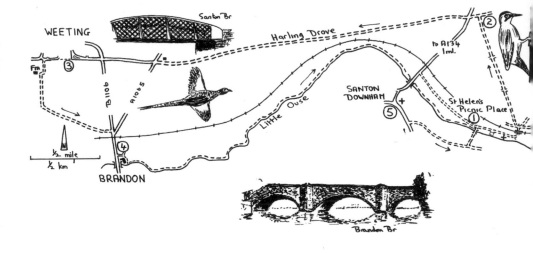

Thetford Forest, now covering over 50,000 acres (20,000 hectares) and Britain's largest lowland pine forest, has been developed from the early plantings in the 1920's when, following the appalling destruction of some half a million acres of woodland taken for the Great War, and much-needed timber had to be imported, the Forestry Commission was set up to produce home-grown timber commercially. They used seed from the original Victorian pine shelter-belts that had been planted in order to try to stabilise the soil and prevent the great sandstorms that overwhelmed Breckland villages like Santon in the Middle Ages – the result of overgrazing this poor quality land by sheep and rabbits. Start from the St Helen's Picnic Place car park (charge) (Ref. 144/826874). This is situated off a minor road just north of Santon Downham.

1) Walk east along the main track, past the fenced site of the old hamlet of Santon – note the interesting information board about the mediaeval village, the church and fair. Pass tiny All Saints and, where the track forks, bear left to pass under the railway. This is the Norwich to Ely line (via Thetford and Brandon). Beyond, cross a firm track and take the left fork (beside the signpost). Follow this grassy 'ride' as it climbs gently out of the valley of the Little Ouse and passes coloured waymarks and cross tracks. The woods here are not a monotonous, gloomy place but blocks of trees at all stages and ages of growth. Pass an information board about the Thetford Rare Birds. Keep ahead along this track to a T-junction, where the main Harling Drove crosses.

2) Turn left along this ancient track. Pre-Roman and later Romanised, this track (The Great Fen Road) led eastward, from the Fens, through Santon Warren, to cross Icknield Way and Peddar's Way toward Roudham. Later it became an important drovers' road. Follow this pleasant track west and almost immediately cross a country lane. Beyond continue for nearly two miles and, just past a long belt of grey-trunk beech trees, and then Bromehill Cottages, cross the busy A1065. Keep ahead along the lane. At the next junction cross (Bll06) into Rectory Lane. Follow this past bungalows and, where it bends right, by a small triangular green, keep to the left of the green to a narrow, signposted pathway next to The Old Rectory gateway.

3) Wind along this walled pathway and follow the estate road ahead for a further 200-yards to just before a junction with a road. Here turn left along a track that winds past Fengate Farm. The track then bears left and passes an industrial estate to a main road. Turn right, and immediately cross the railway. For the most part the Little Ouse marks the county boundary and thus Brandon stands in Suffolk. However, a small administrative loop crosses the river to encompass Brandon railway station! Follow the main road toward Brandon town centre,

and pass the Brandon House Hotel and the Ram Hotel to the old bridge. Brandon town centre is just a further quarter mile. Built on flint, and mainly of flint, Brandon has been the home to England's oldest industry for many, many centuries. The early arrowheads and axes fashioned at the Neolithic flint mines of nearby Grimes Graves, gun flints produced for the Napoleonic Wars, and even the 20th century flints for muzzle-loaders in Africa and North America were produced here!

4) By the bridge turn left into Riverside Way and, passing a modern development of flats, follow the signpost and waymarks rightward down a narrow path to the river. At the Little Ouse turn left to follow this most pleasant riverside path east toward Santon Downham. This path, about two miles long, was for many years impassable because of overgrowth and, more challenging, missing footbridges over the ditches. Due to the resolute persistence, campaigning, and work of a few dedicated and obstinate ramblers there are now fine footbridges and a clear way. At the white-latticed bridge, turn right and cross. Follow the short distance into Santon Downham and by the car-park, toilets and village shop bear left up the hill to pass the 'Church in the Forest', St Mary the Virgin.

5) At the main road keep left along the verge past the churchyard wall for about 200 yards to a signpost and waymarks. Turn left down a sandy track and follow for about 600 yards to railed fields on your left. Pass the first and turn left along the wide, railed trackway between them. This leads back over the Little Ouse to the start.

12 – Lopham Fen and Redgrave

9 Miles

to
A1066

to A1066

to
(B1113)

Low Common Rd.

Visitor
Centre

① REDGRAVE &
LOPHAM FEN N.N.R.

Hide

R. Waveney

②

Water
Works

B1113

⑤

④

Holiday
Farm

Wash Lane

Cowfen Lane

REDGRAVE

③

B1113

N

½ mile

½ km.

This walk starts at the Nature Reserve Visitor Centre (Ref. 144/053803), 1 mile SE of South Lopham and close to the Norfolk/ Suffolk Boundary. Redgrave and Lopham Fen is a National Nature Reserve and one of the most important wetlands in Europe, it is the home of the rare fen raft spider. Tarpan horses, introduced to help control invasive scrub vegetation, graze much of the Fen. The Fen is open daily, the Visitor Centre is open weekends and bank holiday Mondays, plus Tuesday to Friday during school holidays. The walk starts and finishes in Norfolk with most of it in Suffolk. It includes a little of the Angles Way, the 78 mile trail from Great Yarmouth to Knettishall Heath. The fen landscape is contrasted by the undulating farmland to the south, with wide views and some fine old hedges.

1) From the car park go through the gate to the left of the Visitor Centre, then through the first gate on the left. Follow the track, going right at a fork, through the gate at its end and turn left. Do not cross the bridge over the sluice, but continue along the river bank for half a mile to another bridge over the River Waveney, cross and follow the path to a road.

2) Turn left, then right with the road, when it turns to the left go ahead onto a track. When the track turns away from the field edge maintain your direction over a ditch and go ahead across a field, then a grassy field edge path to a road. Turn right and continue just beyond Redgrave Church to turn left onto a field edge path, then right on a track leading to a minor road on the edge of Redgrave village. Follow the road to just beyond the "30" sign and turn left on a grassy track.

3) Cross a road onto a firm track bearing right, keep left on the track at a path junction. Ignore a track on right then shortly turn right onto a public footpath. Follow this track to crossing paths and go ahead over a concrete culvert and around right hand bend, then take a bridleway to the right. Go over a sleeper bridge and bear right onto Cowfen Lane. Turn left onto Wash Lane. Where the road goes left turn sharp right onto a byway across the fields and, when this swings to the right, go ahead on a footpath, then continue in line along a field edge to a road and turn right.

4) Just before reaching Holiday Farm (on your right) turn left on a byway. At the end of the wire fence on your right and on reaching a crossing path, with Angles Way waymarks, turn right. Continue along the edge of Hindercley Fen, then follow a short meandering path through woodland to cross a bridge and continue along a boundary, turning right with the track and out to a road. Turn left and go ahead over crossroads. Just before a slight bend in the road go left on a crossing track.

5) Follow the track through two gates into Redgrave Fen and round to the right. Shortly after a waterworks on your right and immediately before a gate in a crossing fence turn left on a track. Cross a bridge and continue ahead. Pass a bird hide and turn right behind it. Follow the track back to the Visitor Centre.

13 – Yarmouth and Burgh Castle

9¹/₂ Miles

GREAT YARMOU

Weavers Way

A47

Angles Way

R. Yare

Breydon Water

Pumphouse

R. Yare

R. Waveney

Queen's Head Inn

Crow's Fm.

Burgh Castle 'GARIANNONVM'

N
¹/₂ mile
¹/₂ km

This walk starts and finishes at Great Yarmouth Railway Station, which is also served by busses, (Ref. 134/519081) making it ideal for a car free ramble. Car drivers have permission to park in the ASDA car park in the spaces against the riverbank.

1) Leave the station yard by crossing the iron suspension bridge in the SE corner across the River Bure. There are several information boards at this point which is the junction of the Weavers Way and the Angles Way. Turn right along the road and follow it as far as the Haven Bridge on the right hand side. Over the bridge turn right by the Haven Bridge Hotel along a busy street. Where Steam Mill Lane bears round to the left take the narrow footpath straight ahead. Carry on ahead along Critters Road and continue along a gravel path to a tarmac road. Turn right and follow the path beneath the Breydon Bridge. This relatively new structure can be raised to allow tall ships to pass underneath.

2) The path now follows the edge of Breydon Water along the Angles Way for the next 3 miles. To the right the pleasure boats follow the channel of the River Yare whilst the broad tidal mud flats provide a feeding place for birds. Bird watchers will enjoy the many ducks and geese as well as Herons, Warblers, Cormorants and Skylarks. To the left the marshes rely on pumps for their drainage. A brick pumphouse about halfway along the path is the modern replacement for the windpump, the derelict stumps of which are scattered on the skyline. The marshes are home to numerous wild flowers and butterflies. The mud flats of Breydon Water narrow where the River Yare turns south and divides. The Yare turns west towards Norwich whilst the Waveney heads south towards Beccles. Eventually the path reaches the Church Farm Country Club and enters a wooded area.

3) Pass through a gate and immediately turn right through the wood. In about 200 yards climb the wooden steps on the left. At the top turn right and carry on ahead to the walls of Burgh Castle. The castle dates from AD 280. The massive walls of the Roman Castle are present on three sides of the original seven acre rectangular enclosure, the fourth wall has either fallen away down the steep banks of the River Waveney, or been deliberately undermined as part of a later Norman fortification. Layers of red tile reinforce the original flint Roman walls. The solid round bastions are a later addition built as reinforcement. Leave the castle ruins through a gap in the south wall and turn left onto a path between the walls and a hedge. At the end of the field turn left and follow the path to the church. This is one of Norfolk's round towered churches which was almost certainly thatched at one time. At the church turn right along the tarmac road. In 500 yards the Queens Head Inn welcomes weary walkers half way along their route.

4) Continue along the road to a point where it bears sharp right (a mile from the church). Turn left down the farm track and then right towards Crow's Farm. At the farm turn right through a gate and then left alongside the hedge to a kissing gate. Follow the path along the next field with the hedge to the right. Continue straight ahead towards buildings amongst trees. At the farm buildings turn left down a track and almost immediately right and in a few yards turn left and right again. At the edge of the industrial area turn left along a track. Follow the path on the right keeping the perimeter fence on the right as far as a footbridge leading onto the busy road. Turn left and in less than 100 yards cross the road to enter a footpath opposite between factory sites.

5) At a tarmac road turn right and then left into Boundry Road. Continue along the road through the industrial estate and cross the footbridge. The scenery here is in sharp contrast to the earlier part of the walk and reflects the importance of shipping and oil exploration to the town. Continue ahead to a road junction. At Bollard Quay turn left and continue past several sets of traffic lights to the Two Brewers Hotel. Turn right to cross the Haven Bridge and turn left to retrace the route back to the station.

14 – Hethersett and Kett's Oak

9¹/₂ Miles

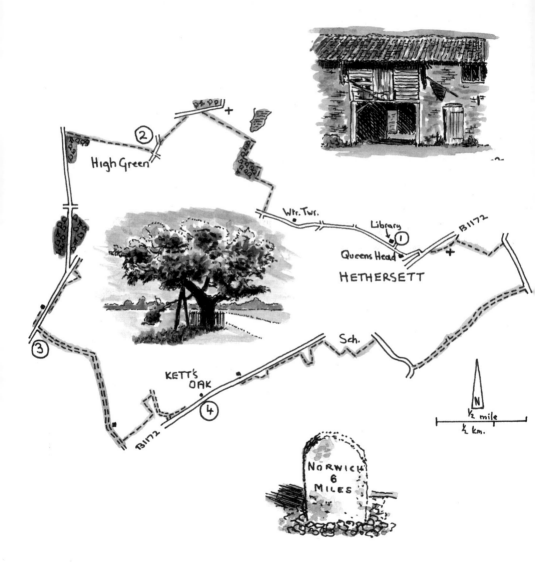

High Green

②

Wtr. Twr.

Library

①

B1172

Queens Head

+

HETHERSETT

③

Sch.

KETT'S OAK

④

B1172

N

¹/₂ mile

¹/₂ km.

NORWICH 6 MILES

Hethersett, lying between Norwich and Wymondham, was for many years a no-go area for walkers. The busy A11 and the lack of footpaths made it an unattractive venue. Today, with the A11 dual carriageway taking the traffic away from the village and some new paths opened up under the Countryside Stewardship Scheme, the area is once more a pleasant place for walkers. Park in one of the many side streets and start the walk from the library in Queen's Road (Ref. 144/157049)

1) With the library on the right walk along Queen's Road in a northwesterly direction. In half a mile pass the water tower on the right and continue along the road to the end of the built up area. Turn right along the footpath opposite the Wymondham road on the left. At the end of the field follow the path to the left. Cross into the next field and follow the path keeping the wooded area to the left. Just before the overhead power lines turn left heading towards a lake and follow the path as far as the tarmac road. At this point it is worthwhile making the short diversion to the Church of All Saints and Saint Mary, Great Melton. The remains of the much older tower of St Mary's stands in the churchyard of the more recent church with its own tower. Turn back along the road past the path and in 100 yards take the crossfield path to the left. Turn left along the road as far as High Green.

2) At the road junction take the footpath on the right opposite the wooden Millenium memorial. At the farmyard follow the path keeping the hedge to the right. Go through a small wood to a tarmac road. Turn left along the road and follow it, over a crossroads and through woods to the junction with Melton Road. Straight ahead there is a gap into a field with a Stewardship Map showing the extent of the public access. Follow the signed path around a group of bushes to the right and back around them to a headland alongside the road. At a group of buildings the signed path crosses the road and continues in the same direction in the opposite field. Keep to the road side of the deep ditch and in a few yards take the farm road on the left.

3) Follow this track for about ³/₄ mile either on the hard track or the optional grass headlands alongside it which are part of the Stewardship Scheme. Pass by the buildings of Carpenters Farm and at the end of the next field turn left along another grass headland. At the corner of the field turn left and in 100 yards turn right over a bridge. At the farm track turn right and follow the track to the farm buildings. Immediately before the main road turn left along the field margin as far as the Stewardship path allows. Leave the field and turn left along the road to Ketts' Oak.

4) In July 1549 the brothers Robert and William Kett met under this tree with a group of common holders to demonstrate against the practice of enclosing common land. Their protest became a revolt and ended with the death of thousands of rebels in a pitched battle with 10,000 troops just outside Norwich. Both brothers were hanged for their part in the revolt. Continue along the old A11 towards Hethersett, as far as a layby on the right opposite a used car sales area. Cross over to the layby and go through a gate into another Stewardship Scheme. Turn left and follow the stewardship path parallel to the road. Follow the path as it follows the field margins as they wind around the rear of properties along the road. At the edge of the grounds of Old Hall School follow the path to the right keeping the grounds to the left. Just before the end of the playing field turn left into the playing field and immediately right alongside the hedge. Keep on the path as far as the Ketteringham Road. Turn right along the road and about halfway around a long right-hand bend take the broad track to the left. Keep on this track for about ³/₄ mile until it joins a tarmac road. Turn left and at the bottom of the hill take the footpath over a stile on the left. Follow the path over a series of stiles as far as the Church. Carry on the path straight through the churchyard to rejoin the main road close to the village sign. Cross the road and take the road to the left as far as the Queen's Head. Turn right at the pub to return to the starting point.

15 – Bridgham Lane

10 Miles

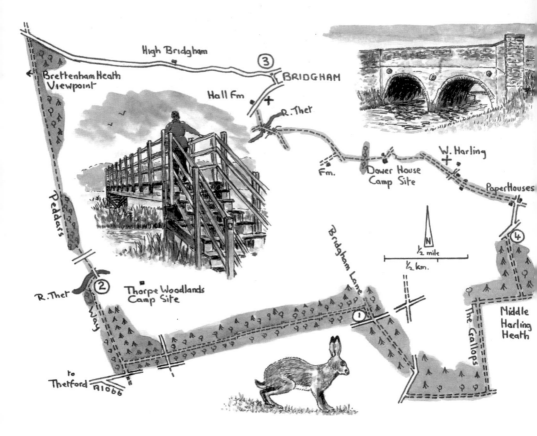

This walk includes forest, Breckland heath and part of the Peddars Way. It starts at Bridgham Lane Picnic Site (Ref. 144/968837).

When walking in any part of Thetford Forest you should be aware that you might find sections closed from time to time because of forestry operations – it is a working environment. It will usually be possible to find a safe and peaceful alternative route.

1) Walk a short distance from the road and just at the end of the parking area take the first track to the left. Ignore all crossing tracks, including the tarmac track to the Thorpe Woodlands Camp Site. At the Peddars Way along the edge of the woods turn right and follow the Way to the River Thet and bridge. Until the middle of 20th century there were remains of a Roman ford crossing the river near this point.

2) Go over the bridge and soon across a road, continuing along the Peddars Way. You should be able to see traces of the Roman agger, the embankment forming the foundations of the road, although the origins of Peddars Way are pre-Roman. It was the northeastern section of a system of pre-historic track ways, which stretched from The Wash to the Dorset coast via routes similar to the paths we now know as the Icknield Way, the Ridgeway, and the Wessex Way. About three quarters of a mile from the road you will reach Brettenham Heath Nature Reserve and at this point pass through the remains of a wire fence onto a parallel track. Access to the reserve was formerly by permit only, but is now open for at least part of the year under the new access provisions. It is partially visible from the track and there is a viewpoint. It is an example of dry Breckland heath, until the planting of Thetford Forest this land-scape would have been typical of the area. Trees and scrub are kept at bay by grazing and it is a haven for curlews, lapwing, butterflies, flowering plants and grasses. At the road turn right (just left of this point is the entrance to the Nature Reserve) and continue to Bridgham (there is no shop or pub in the village). Nelson would have visited Bridgham when he was a boy, an uncle was rector at the church.

3) At the junction keep right and right again along The Street. Pass the church, then, just beyond and opposite Hall Farm go left on a footpath across a meadow, over a footbridge to a track and left over a brick bridge. Immediately after a second brick bridge turn left over a stile, through trees and bear right to a second stile. Go ahead with a fence on your right, over a third stile, continue to a field corner and bear right through a gap. Continue on a right edge to meet a track from the right. Go ahead through two wooden gates and a metal gate, then shortly left on a footpath across a field. Cross a footbridge, through trees and across Dower House Camp Site. Go under a trellis arch between the house and shower block, then

bear slightly left onto a wide track through the trees, but after a few yards turn right at a waymark, follow white arrows on trees and soon left at another waymark to find a pair of knobbed gateposts in a fence. Pass through onto a clear path and follow this to emerge near West Harling Church. If you wish you may go across the field to the church, now redundant, it is cared for by the Churches Conservation Trust, it is usually locked and is used only occasionally. The churchyard can be a pleasant place to stop for a little while. The forest swallowed up the sites of hall and village in the 1930s, now there are just a few houses nearby. West Harling Hall, a grand Georgian house with extensive pleasure grounds, was built in 1725 and demolished in 1931. It had replaced an older house, probably built in the early fifteenth century. Recently a large new house has been built close to the site. Way over to the north, near the river is the site of an Iron Age settlement at Micklemoor Hill. Perhaps there have been fewer people living around here in the last three-quarters of a century than there were in thousands of years before? Turn right on (or rejoin) the track and follow to the road at Paper Houses, turn right and then right again at a junction.

4) Go left on the first track, through a small parking place, continue straight until you reach a gate and Middle Harling Heath, which is being restored to Breckland vegetation. Turn right along the outside of the fence, at the next junction go left along The Gallops – a broad track lined with some venerable old trees. (Perhaps it was part of an avenue leading to West Harling Hall, the alignment is correct?) Continue to the end and then go right along the edge of the forest to a road and turn right. Soon, as the road bends to the left, turn left onto a track, which will lead you to the road and directly opposite Bridgham Lane and your starting point.

16 – Stokesby and Acle

11 Miles

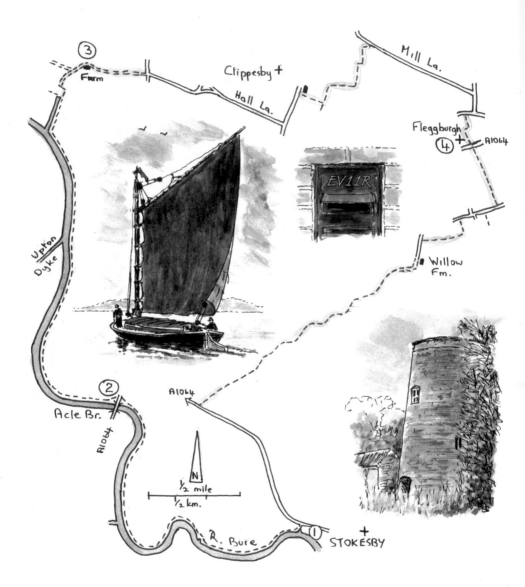

Clippesby +

Mill La.

③ Farm

Hall La.

Fleggburgh
④ + A1064

EV11R

Willow Fm.

Upton Dyke

A1064

② Acle Br.

A1064

N

½ mile
½ km.

R. Bure

① STOKESBY +